PIANO · VOCAL · GUITAR

THIRD DAY WIRE

ISBN 0-634-08146-2

HAL•LEONARD® CORPORATION

7777 W. BLUEMOUND RD. P.O. BOX 13819 MILWAUKEE, WI 53213

Visit Hal Leonard Online at
www.halleonard.com

'TIL THE DAY I DIE

Words by MAC POWELL
Music by TAI ANDERSON, BRAD AVERY,
DAVID CARR, MARK LEE and MAC POWELL

I wan-na tell____ you,
I said, "for - ev - er,"

I wan-na tell____ you just____ how I____ feel.
I said, "for - ev - er," and ___ I mean ___ it.

Recorded a half step higher.

COME ON BACK TO ME

Words by MAC POWELL
Music by TAI ANDERSON, BRAD AVERY,
DAVID CARR, MARK LEE and MAC POWELL

Moderately

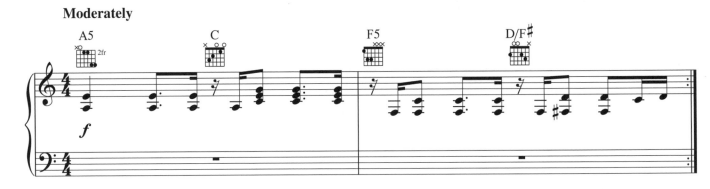

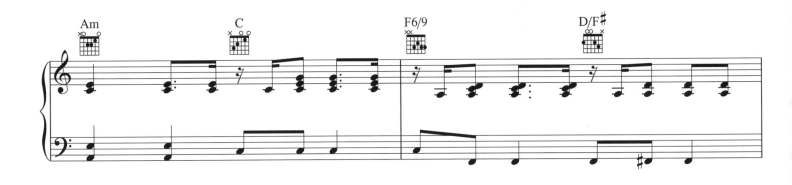

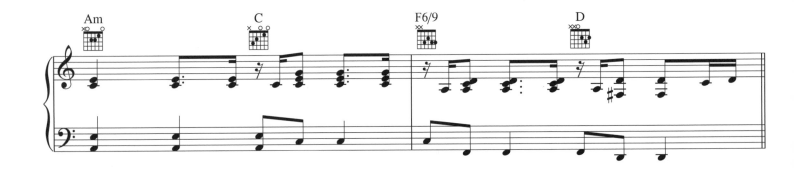

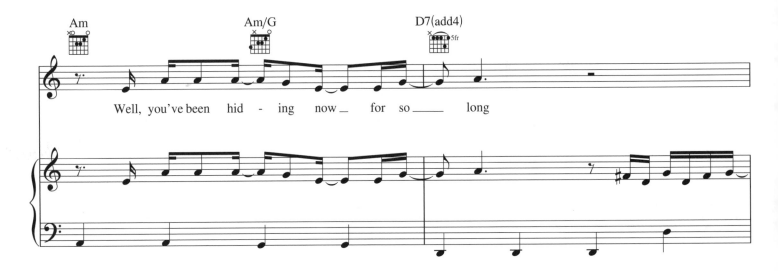

Well, you've been hid - ing now ___ for so ___ long

WIRE

Words by MARK LEE
Music by TAI ANDERSON, BRAD AVERY,
DAVID CARR, MARK LEE and MAC POWELL

ROCKSTAR

Words by MAC POWELL
Music by TAI ANDERSON, BRAD AVERY,
DAVID CARR, MARK LEE and MAC POWELL

I BELIEVE

Words by MAC POWELL
Music by TAI ANDERSON, BRAD AVERY,
DAVID CARR, MARK LEE and MAC POWELL

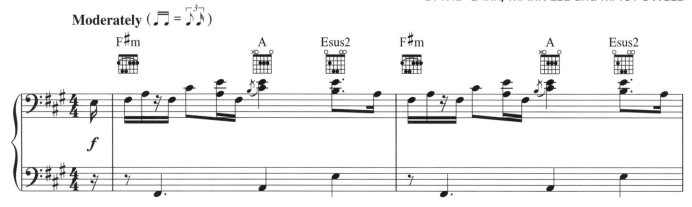

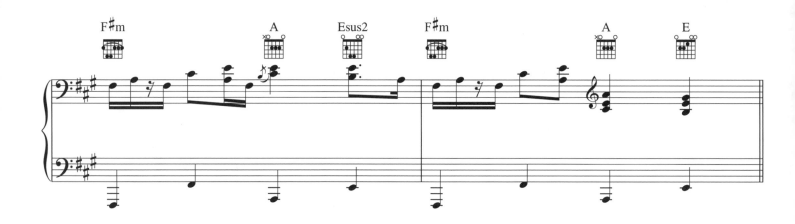

Give me some - thing that ___ I can be - lieve ___ and then ___ I'll ___

And if I had ___ the strength ___ to move a moun - tain, would You ___

IT'S A SHAME

Words by MAC POWELL
Music by TAI ANDERSON, BRAD AVERY,
DAVID CARR, MARK LEE and MAC POWELL

* *Recorded a half step higher.*

BLIND

Words by MAC POWELL
Music by TAI ANDERSON, BRAD AVERY,
DAVID CARR, MARK LEE and MAC POWELL

*Recorded a half step higher.

How could I have been so blind?

How could I have been so blind?

How could I have been so blind?

I GOT A FEELING

Words by MAC POWELL
Music by TAI ANDERSON, BRAD AVERY,
DAVID CARR, MARK LEE and MAC POWELL

Moderately fast

I got a mes - sage, I got a song.
I got a mis - sion, I got a sign.

Can I get a wit - ness? Tell me what's go - ing ____ on. ____
Is an - y - bod - y lis - t'ning? I got - ta make sure this ____ time. ____

____ I'll show the peo - ple ____ a bet - ter way. ____
____ I'll tell the peo - ple ____ what's on my mind. ____

YOU ARE MINE

Words by MAC POWELL
Music by TAI ANDERSON, BRAD AVERY,
DAVID CARR, MARK LEE and MAC POWELL

INNOCENT

Words by MARK LEE
Music by TAI ANDERSON, BRAD AVERY,
DAVID CARR, MARK LEE and MAC POWELL

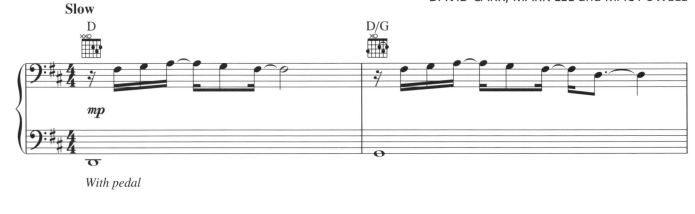

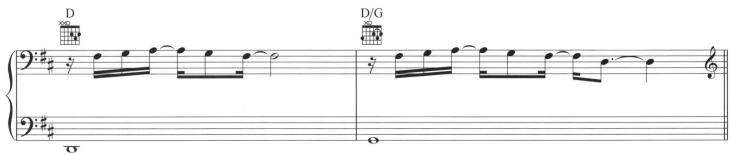

It seemed like I'd run out of sec - ond chanc - es

and they sen - tenced me to die.

I am in - no - cent ___ and I ___ have been ___ set free. ___

___ I no long - er ___ have chains a - round ___ my feet. ___

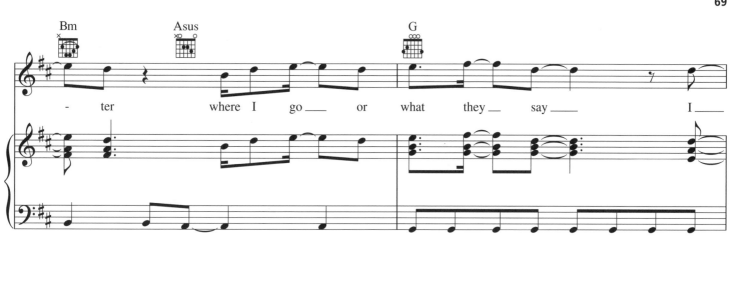

-ter where I go ___ or what they ___ say ___ I ___

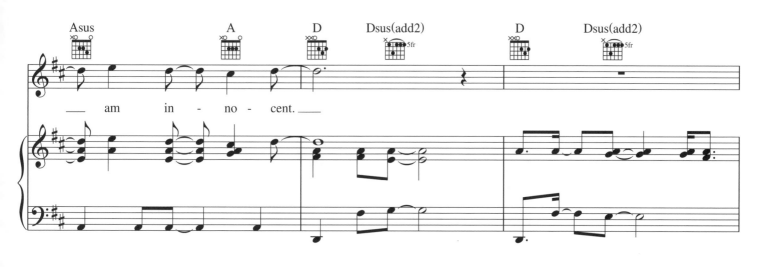

___ am in - no - cent. ___

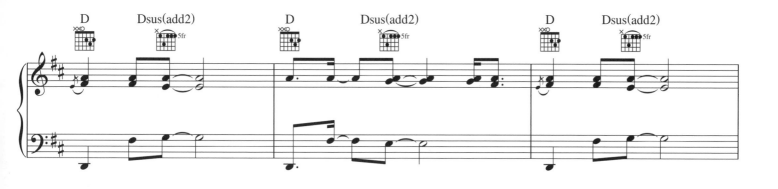

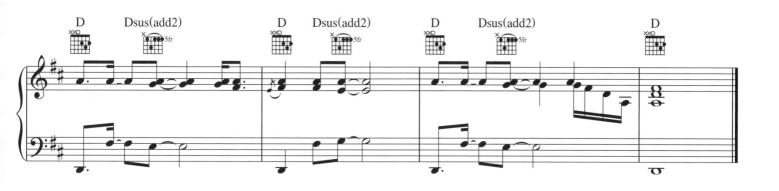

BILLY BROWN

Words by MAC POWELL
Music by TAI ANDERSON, BRAD AVERY,
DAVID CARR, MARK LEE and MAC POWELL

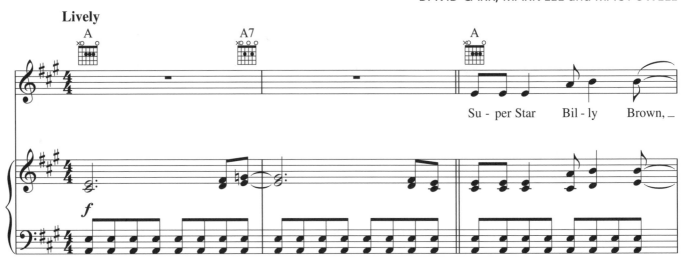

Su - per Star Bil - ly Brown, _

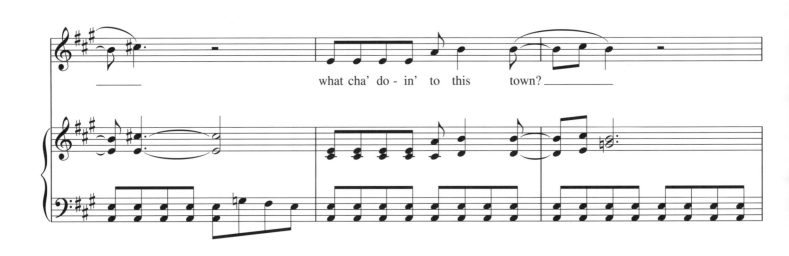

what cha' do - in' to this town? _

Don't you know that ev - 'ry - bod - y here _ wants to be like _ you. _

SAN ANGELO

Words by MAC POWELL
Music by TAI ANDERSON, BRAD AVERY,
DAVID CARR, MARK LEE and MAC POWELL

I WILL HOLD MY HEAD HIGH

Words by MARK LEE
Music by TAI ANDERSON, BRAD AVERY,
DAVID CARR, MARK LEE and MAC POWELL

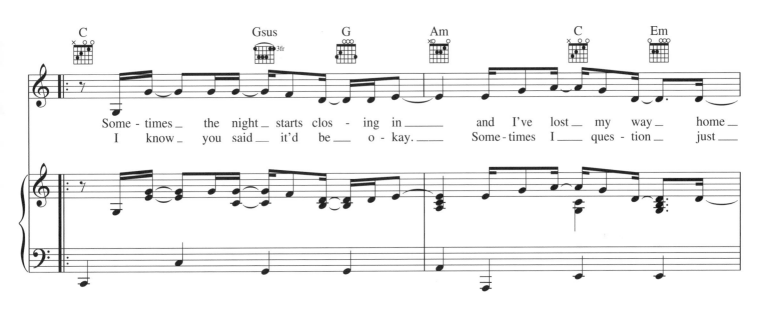

Some-times the night starts clos-ing in and I've lost my way home
I know you said it'd be o-kay. Some-times I ques-tion just

a-gain. I'm run-ning out of plac-es I can turn.
the same. I won-der if my prob-lems are too small.

More Contemporary Christian Folios from Hal Leonard

AVALON – THE CREED
Our matching folio to the very latest from this popular CCM vocal quartet features photos and all ten songs: Abundantly • All • Be with You • The Creed • Far Away from Here • The Good Way • I Bring It to You • Overjoyed • Renew Me • You Were There.

_____00306601 Piano/Vocal/Guitar........ $14.95

WAIT FOR ME – THE BEST FROM REBECCA ST. JAMES
Our matching folio to the first best-of compilation from Aussie gospel artist Rebecca St. James includes 16 previously recorded songs: Breathe • God • Here I Am • I Thank You • Lamb of God • Mirror • Pray • Psalm 139 • Reborn • Song of Love • Speak to Me • Stand • Wait for Me • and more.

_____00306546 Piano/Vocal/Guitar........ $14.95

JEREMY CAMP – STAY
The _All Music Guide_ says CCM newcomer Jeremy Camp "delivers one of the most awe-inspiring performances of any debut CCM artist in the past decade" and calls _Stay_ "vocally, musically and lyrically ... a potent mix of one standout cut after another." Our matching folio features all 12 tracks: All the Time • Breaking My Fall • In Your Presence • Nothing • Right Here • Stay • Take My Life • Understand • Walk by Faith • and more.

_____00306565 Piano/Vocal/Guitar........ $14.95

KEITH GREEN – THE ULTIMATE COLLECTION
Our 20-song collection matches Sparrow's latest compilation CD of the late, great Keith Green, who died in a plane crash in 1982. Includes: Asleep in the Light • I Can't Believe It • I Want to Be More like Jesus • Jesus Commands Us to Go • Make My Life a Prayer to You • My Eyes Are Dry • Oh Lord, You're Beautiful • Pledge My Head to Heaven • Rushing Wind • Soften Your Heart • There Is a Redeemer • You Are the One• You! • Your Love Broke Through • and more.

_____00306518 Piano/Vocal/Guitar........ $16.95

JENNIFER KNAPP – THE WAY I AM
Includes all 12 tunes from the critically acclaimed CD: Around Me • Breathe on Me • By and By • Charity • Come to Me • Fall Down • In Two (The Lament) • Light of the World • No Regrets • Say Won't You Say • Sing Mary Sing • The Way I Am.

00306467 Piano/Vocal/Guitar................. $14.95

TWILA PARIS – HOUSE OF WORSHIP
Includes 12 songs : Christ in Us • Come Emmanuel • Fill My Heart • For Eternity • Glory and Honor • God of All • I Want the World to Know • Make Us One • Not My Own • We Bow Down • We Will Glorify • You Are God..

_____00306517Piano/Vocal/Guitar........ $14.95

JEFF DEYO – LIGHT
All 13 songs from the second solo release by the former Sonicflood frontman: As I Lift You Up • Bless the Lord • I Am Yours Forever • I Fear You • I Love You • Keep My Heart • Ray of Light • Sacrifice of Praise • Show the Wonder • Take Me to You • These Hands • We Come to Your Throne • Your Name Is Holy.

_____00306603 Piano/Vocal/Guitar........ $14.95

CASTING CROWNS
Matching folio to the Steven Curtis Chapman-produced eponymous debut from this adult contemporary Gospel group. Features 10 songs: American Dream • Glory • Here I Go Again • If We Are the Body • Life of Praise • Praise You with the Dance • Voice of Truth • What If His People Prayed • Who Am I • Your Love Is Extravagant.

_____00306621 Piano/Vocal/Guitar........ $14.95

BETHANY DILLON
All 11 songs from the self-titled Sparrow CD from this critically acclaimed 15-year-old singer/songwriter: Aimless • All I Need • Beautiful • Exodus • For My Love • Great Big Mystery • Lead Me On • Move Forward • Revolutionaries • A Voice Calling Out • Why.

_____00306636Piano/Vocal/Guitar........ $14.95

PHILLIPS, CRAIG AND DEAN – LET YOUR GLORY FALL
Our matching folio features all ten inspirational tunes from this popular CCM trio's 2003 release: Every Day • Fall Down • Hallelujah (Your Love Is Amazing) • Here I Am to Worship • How Deep the Father's Love for Us • Lord, Let Your Glory Fall • My Praise • Only You • What Kind of Love Is This • The Wonderful Cross.

_____00306519 Piano/Vocal/Guitar........ $14.95

NICHOLE NORDEMAN – WOVEN & SPUN
Includes all 11 songs from the 2002 release of this Dove Award nominee: Doxology • Even Then • Gratitude • Healed • Holy • I Am • Legacy • Mercies New • My Offering • Never Loved You More • Take Me As I Am.

_____00306494 Piano/Vocal/Guitar........ $14.95

ZOEGIRL – DIFFERENT KIND OF FREE
Our matching folio features all 11 songs: Beautiful Name • Contagious • Different Kind of Free • Feel Alright • Inside Out • Life to Me • Love Me for Me • She • Unbroken • Wait • You Get Me.

00306562 Piano/Vocal/Guitar............... $14.95

SONGS FROM !HERO THE ROCK OPERA
Selections from the popular touring musical that asks the question, "What if Jesus had been born in Bethlehem ... Pennsylvania?" This folio presents 15 selections from this modern-day version of the greatest story ever told. Songs, by today's most popular CCM artists, include: Fire of Love • Hero • I Am • Kill the Hero • Lose My Life with You • Manna from Heaven • Raised in Harlem • Secrets of the Heart • and more.

_____00306634 Piano/Vocal/Guitar........ $14.95

THIRD DAY: WIRE
13 songs: Billy Brown • Blind • Come On Back to Me • I Believe • I Got a Feeling • I Will Hold My Head High • Innocent • It's a Shame • Rock Star • San Angelo • 'Til the Day I Die • Wire • You Are Mine.

_____00306629 Piano/Vocal/Guitar........ $14.95

DC TALK – INTERMISSION: THE GREATEST HITS
17 of DC Talk's best: Between You and Me • Chance • Colored People • Consume Me • Hardway (Remix) • I Wish We'd All Been Ready • In the Light • Jesus Freak • Jesus Is Just Alright • Luv Is a Verb • Mind's Eye • My Will • Say the Words (Now) • Socially Acceptable • SugarCoat It • Supernatural • What If I Stumble.

_____00306414 Piano/Vocal/Guitar........ $14.95

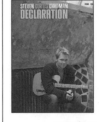

STEVEN CURTIS CHAPMAN – DECLARATION
13 songs: Bring It On • Carry You to Jesus • Declaration of Dependence • God Follower • God Is God • Jesus Is Life • Live Out Loud • Magnificent Obsession • No Greater Love • Savior • See the Glory • This Day • When Love Takes You In.

_____00306453 Piano/Vocal/Guitar........ $14.95

SWITCHFOOT – THE BEAUTIFUL LETDOWN
All 11 songs from the CD by these San Diego-based Christian alt-rockers: Adding to the Noise • Ammunition • Beautiful Letdown • Dare You to Move • Gone • Meant to Live • More Than Fine • On Fire • Redemption Side • This Is Your Life • Twenty-Four.

_____00306547 Piano/Vocal/Guitar........ $14.95

0804